Forest House

MW01121707

DISCARD

DISCARD

DATE DUE				
JUN 2 5 1997	8379			
JUL 1 7 1997	4792			
APR 1 4 199	3670			
MAR 2 9 2000	6898			
AUG 1 6 2002	9962			
OCT 2 8 2003	9850			
OCT 2 2 '08				

DEMCO 25-370

A Guide to Its Care and Display

by

Ruth Shaw Radlauer

Design and illustration
by J.J. Smith-Moore

FOREST HOUSE ™

Forest House Publishing Company, Inc.
Lake Forest, Illinois

Produced by Radlauer Productions,

Incorporated for

Forest House Publishing Company, Incorporated.

Photo Credits: page 4, National Aeronautics and Space Administration; page 9, National Heritage Arts; page 33, Robin Radlauer.

Music manuscript, page 40 produced by Thomas Griep

Library of Congress Cataloging-in-Publication Data

Radlauer, Ruth. 1926-
Honor the flag : a guide to its care and display / by Ruth Shaw Radlauer : design and illustration by J.J. Smith-Moore.
     p.   cm.
   Includes index.
   ISBN 1-878363-61-1 (lib. bdg.)
   1. Flags--United States--History--Juvenile literature.
[1. Flags--United States.] I. Smith-Moore, J. J., 1955- ill.
II. Title.
CR113.R33 1996
929.9'2' 0973--dc20   96-5399
                                                    CIP
                                                    AC

CONTENTS

On August 1, 1971, Apollo 15 EVA (extravehicular activity module) landed about three miles from the base of the moon mountain called Hadley Delta. Astronaut David R. Scott photographed James B. Irwin as he saluted the U.S. flag raised on that day. Partly visible is the Lunar Module "Falcon."

Two years before this on, July 20, 1969, Neil A. Armstrong, and Edwin E. Aldrin, Jr. had planted a U.S. flag on the moon. It was the first banner of any nation ever to reach the moon.

HONOR THE FLAG

Old Glory, the Stars and Stripes, the Red, White, and Blue, Star-Spangled Banner: no matter what you call it, the United States flag is a symbol of our land. It means many things to many people, and there are ways you can honor this proud banner that flies over our free country.

Just as you use certain manners at a party and different ones at a baseball game, there are manners or ways we honor and take care of the national flag.

Rules that tell what to do and not do with the flag are called the *code*. Since 1942, we have had an official code that tells us how to treat our flag. Today we follow the code under Public Law 344, approved July 7, 1976, by the 94th Congress.

WHERE THE FLAG FLIES

The United States flag doesn't fly the way an eagle flies. We say it flies when we raise the flag over or near public buildings, schools, ships at sea, and other places outdoors.

We show, or display, the flag indoors, too. Because the flag is special, there are special ways to display it and take care of it.

We honor the flag when we follow the code for its use and display.

We fly our banner, but the flag itself also *has* a *fly,* which is the measurement of its length. As the diagram shows, the striped end of the flag is called the *fly,* too.

Look at the diagram to find out what some other flag words mean: *hoist, union, canton, pole, staff,* and *peak.*

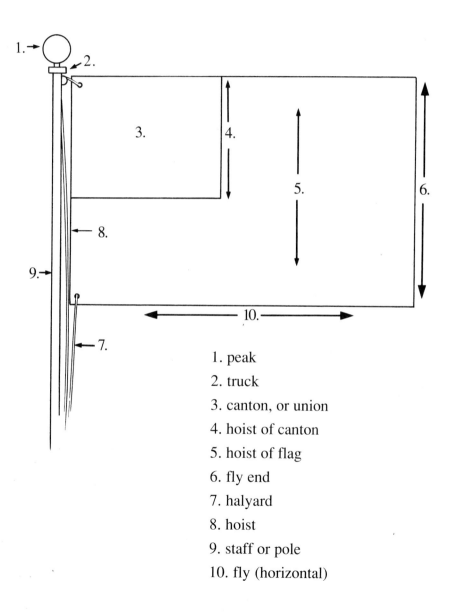

1. peak
2. truck
3. canton, or union
4. hoist of canton
5. hoist of flag
6. fly end
7. halyard
8. hoist
9. staff or pole
10. fly (horizontal)

RAISE THE FLAG

When you raise the Red, White, and Blue on a pole, take care not to let it touch the ground. Clip it on the rope called a *halyard* and raise it quickly. The flag must go to the top of the flagpole without stopping.

Do these same things when the flag is displayed on a pole attached to a building. The flag should always be at the far end of the pole unless it is to fly at half-staff. (See page 14).

The U.S. Marine Corps War Memorial in Washington, D. C. was modeled after a famous photograph taken by Joe Rosenthal. It shows six Marines who raised the flag when the island of Iwo Jima was captured by the U.S. during World War II.

LOWER THE FLAG

Most of the time, the Stars and Stripes are taken down every day before sunset. You *can* fly the flag 24 hours a day if you shine a light on it during the dark hours. To lower the flag, bring it down slowly and smoothly, without stopping.

Again, take care not to let the flag touch the ground. Now it's time to fold our flag in a special way.

HOW TO FOLD THE FLAG

You need a partner to help you fold the flag the right way. If you are the main folder, hold the striped end (the fly) of the flag by two corners. Your partner has the hoist, the end with the stars. This person holds the blue corner in the left hand and a red striped corner in the right hand.

Now, together, you fold the stripes over the blue, with corners meeting. When you fold the flag lengthwise a *second time*, your partner has blue cloth in both hands.

This is the second fold.

Next you fold the corner in your right hand over to meet the left edge.

The corner in your left hand now folds up to meet the left edge.

Then the corner in your left hand goes over to meet the right edge, and the corner in your right hand folds up to meet the right edge again.

Keep folding this way until you have a three-sided, or triangular, blue "package" studded with white stars.

Put the flag away where it will not be torn, soiled, or damaged in any way.

HALF-STAFF

What is a staff, and what is a pole? A staff is a rod on which a flag is carried, as in a parade. A pole stays in one place on the ground or attached to a building.

Whether a flag is on a staff or pole, we sometimes fly it at *half-staff,* or *half-mast,* halfway up the pole. We do this when an important person dies. We show our sadness and respect for the person who has died when we display his or her country's banner at half-staff. For a president, the flag is at half-mast for 30 days. Governors, great generals, past presidents, members of Congress and others: for each of these, the flag is at half-mast for a different length of time.

Even if the flag is to be at half-staff, we still raise it all the way to the top when we put it up. Then we lower the flag slowly to the middle of the pole's length.

At the end of the day, we raise the flag all the way to the top once more before slowly bringing it down to be folded and put away for the night. (The flag can be left out all night if you shine a light on it.)

DARKNESS

Would you feel honored if people left you out in the dark? Of course not, but it might not be so bad if there were a light shining on you. The Flag Code says any American can fly a flag 24 hours a day, but we don't leave it out in the dark.

If you fly the flag at night for a patriotic effect, you must keep it lit with spotlights.

Wherever and whenever our banner flies, citizens want to see it waving proudly.

STORMY WEATHER

Would your friend feel honored if you left her out in a storm? Her clothes would droop and cling to her body, and she'd look sad and uncared for.

We don't treat Old Glory that way, either. If a storm starts after the morning raising of the flag, the code tells us to take it down. Lower the flag and take it inside. If it's wet, you wait until the flag dries before folding it in the special way shown on page 12.

You and your friend *could* stay out in a storm if you wear the right kinds of clothes. So too, if your flag is made of special, *all-weather* cloth, you can display it in a storm.

FADED AND WORN, TATTERED AND TORN

How many times have you seen a flag with ragged edges? Perhaps you've seen a flag with stripes faded to a dull pink. You probably didn't like to see the banner of our land looking so tired and worn.

It may be time to retire a faithful friend and get a new flag with bright blue, clean white, and true red. But what will happen to the old flag?

The code says the flag should not be just thrown away. It should be destroyed or retired in a special or dignified way. The code suggests burning. Even then, we do not let the flag touch anything beneath it.

When a flag is to be burned, it's done carefully by a grown person in a special, private ceremony. A water hose nearby can be used to keep the fire where it belongs.

You might like to write a ceremony with special words you'd like to say as you retire a tattered old flag.

DISPLAY THE FLAG

With Other Flags

When the flags of several nations are displayed, they must all be on separate staffs. All the flags should be about the same size and stand at the same height.

If you show Old Glory with several other flags like state, city, or club flags, it belongs in the middle. It must also stand higher than the rest.

In a Parade

Most parades begin with our nation's flag. Sometimes there are state and city banners in the parade, too. If there are, the American flag goes on the right (the flag's right) with all the other flags in a line to the U.S. flag's left.

The Star-Spangled Banner can also go first, ahead of the center of a lineup of flags. People who carry the flag and walk beside it are called the color or honor guard.

The U.S. flag does not belong on a float unless it is on a staff. It must not be draped over the hood, top, sides, or back of a car, railroad train, or boat. On a car the flag goes on a staff connected to the chassis or it's clamped to the right fender.

Be sure to salute or give special attention when our banner goes by.

The flag is on the speaker's right, but on the left of those in the audience.

In a Big Hall

If our flag is hanging flat against a wall, the blue part, called the union or canton, should be on the flag's right. When you look at the banner, the union is to *your* left. The stripes can go up and down or side to side.

Sometimes two flags have their staffs crossed against a wall. In this case, the American flag is on its own right with its staff in front of the other flag's staff.

A flag on the stage should be hung behind and above the speaker, with the blue to the speaker's right. If it's on a staff, the flag stands to the speaker's right. Any other flag goes on the left.

In a Window

When you stand outside a window where a flag is hanging, the blue union or canton belongs on your left, the flag's own right.

In Terrible Need

If you were in some terrible trouble such as being caught on a cliff with no way to get down, a flag could save you. You can fly a U.S. flag upside down as a signal that you need help. This is the *only* time the stripes would be at the top and the blue canton or union at the bottom.

Over the Street

☆

There's even a code for hanging our flag over the street. It's hung on a line that stretches from one side of the street to the other. We hang it by the hoist with the blue at the top and the stripes going up and down. But which way does the canton go?

If the street goes east and west, the blue canton hangs toward the north. A flag over a street running north and south should have the canton to the east.

Do you suppose this is because the sun rises in the east and we think of the north pole as the top of the world?

On a Casket

☆

Sometimes a flag covers a casket, the box in which a person is buried. When a flag covers a casket, the blue union goes toward the head, over the dead person's left shoulder.

At a funeral, the flag does not go with the casket when it's lowered into the ground. Here again, our banner must not touch the ground. Two people fold the flag and often give it to the closest family member or friend of the dead person.

NO FLAGS HERE

Here are most of the *don'ts* and a few *dos,* some *nevers,* and a *forever* about the United States flag.

Don't use the flag for advertising, and never add advertising signs to the staff or halyard (rope) on which a U.S. flag is flying.

Don't embroider the flag on articles like cushions and handkerchiefs.

Don't print the flag on paper cups, napkins, boxes, or anything to be thrown away. You can use red, blue, and white stripes and stars to decorate such things, but not U.S. flags.

Don't let the flag touch anything beneath it such as the ground, floor, water, table, or things for sale.

Don't throw a flag away as you would a paper sack. Do have a ceremony for a worn-out flag. See pages 20-21.

Don't fly another flag above or higher than the U.S. flag. Do see pages 22-25.

Don't fly the flag in a storm unless it's made of all-weather cloth.

Do shine a spotlight on any flag flown after sunset.

Don't use the flag as a drapery. Do, instead, decorate with red, white, and blue *bunting* with blue at the top and red at the bottom.

Do make the flag an important part of a ceremony when a monument is first shown, but don't cover a monument with our banner

Never carry a flag horizontally or flat except on a casket.

Never add any marks, patches, letters, or anything else to the flag.

Don't wrap or carry things in the flag.

Never use a U.S. flag as clothing.

Forever, let our banner stand tall and wave proudly.

Never use a U.S. flag as clothing. The author found a way to wear the stars and stripes without wearing a flag.

SPECIAL DAYS FOR A SPECIAL FLAG

Fly our country's banner any day, but especially on these days.

January 1—New Year's Day

January 20 every four years—Inauguration Day

January—Third Monday—Martin Luther King's Birthday

February 12—Lincoln's Birthday

February—Third Monday—Washington's Birthday

Easter (in March or April)

May—Second Sunday—Mother's Day

May—Third Saturday—Armed Forces Day

May—Last Monday—Memorial Day (Flag at half-staff until noon)

June—Second Sunday—Father's Day

June 14—Flag Day

July 4—Independence Day

September—First Monday—Labor Day

September 17—Citizenship Day

October—Second Monday—Columbus Day

October 27—Navy Day

November 11—Veteran's Day

November—Fourth Thursday—Thanksgiving Day

December 25—Christmas Day

Other days proclaimed by the President and on state birthdays, usually called admission days and on state holidays.

WHAT THE FLAG MEANS

The first flag, adopted by Congress on June 14, 1777, had thirteen red and white stripes and thirteen white stars in a blue field called the canton or union. The thirteens stood for the first thirteen states.

As new states joined the country, stripes and stars were added until the flag had fifteen stripes and fifteen stars. Then people decided to go back to thirteen stripes and add only stars for each new state. Do you know how many stars are on the flag today?

The colors of the flag have meanings. To some people, red stands for bravery or courage. White is for honesty and cleanliness, and blue means truth and loyalty. Others have said that red is for hardiness (strength) and courage (bravery), white means purity and innocence (clean and unspoiled), and blue stands for vigilance (watchfulness), perseverance (staying power), and justice (fairness).

In the language of flags, stars have always meant power and might. In our flag they also stand for the states. Held together in the blue union, the stars symbolize our many states, banded together in a country called the United States of America.

37

A STAR FOR EACH STATE

Every star in the U.S. flag stands for a state.
Find the star for your state.

1. DELAWARE	26. MICHIGAN
2. PENNSYLVANIA	27. FLORIDA
3. NEW JERSEY	28. TEXAS
4. GEORGIA	29. IOWA
5. CONNECTICUT	30. WISCONSIN
6. MASSACHUSETTS	31. CALIFORNIA
7. MARYLAND	32. MINNESOTA
8. SOUTH CAROLINA	33. OREGON
9. NEW HAMPSHIRE	34. KANSAS
10. VIRGINIA	35. WEST VIRGINIA
11. NEW YORK	36. NEVADA
12. NORTH CAROLINA	37. NEBRASKA
13. RHODE ISLAND	38. COLORADO
14. VERMONT	39. NORTH DAKOTA
15. KENTUCKY	40. SOUTH DAKOTA
16. TENNESSEE	41. MONTANA
17. OHIO	42. WASHINGTON
18. LOUISIANA	43. IDAHO
19. INDIANA	44. WYOMING
20. MISSISSIPPI	45. UTAH
21. ILLINOIS	46. OKLAHOMA
22. ALABAMA	47. NEW MEXICO
23. MAINE	48. ARIZONA
24. MISSOURI	49. ALASKA
25. ARKANSAS	50. HAWAII

6

11

17

22

28

33

39

44

50

The Star Spangled Banner

Words by Francis Scott Key

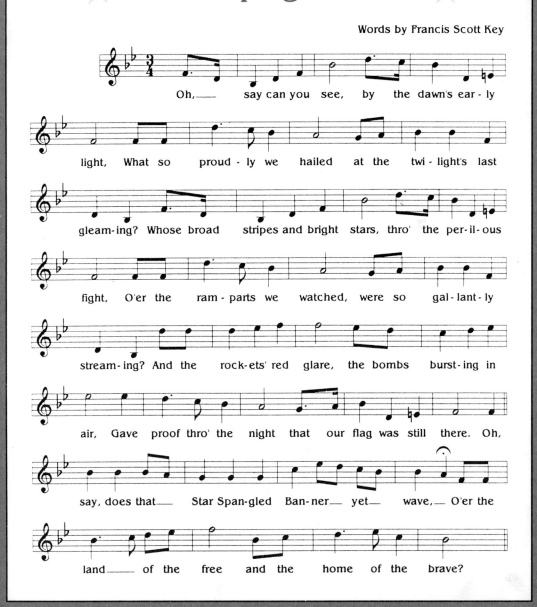

Oh,—— say can you see, by the dawn's ear - ly

light, What so proud - ly we hailed at the twi - light's last

gleam- ing? Whose broad stripes and bright stars, thro' the per - il - ous

fight, O'er the ram - parts we watched, were so gal - lant - ly

stream- ing? And the rock-ets' red glare, the bombs burst-ing in

air, Gave proof thro' the night that our flag was still there. Oh,

say, does that—— Star Span-gled Ban-ner—— yet—— wave,—— O'er the

land—— of the free and the home of the brave?

THE NATIONAL ANTHEM

The words for the National Anthem were written by Francis Scott Key. During the War of 1812, he was held prisoner all night on a British ship. During that time, a fleet of British ships bombarded Fort McHenry for many hours. This fort protected Baltimore, Maryland.

The next morning Mr. Key didn't know whether or not the fort had fallen. Then he saw a huge American flag still flying over the walls of the fort. He was so excited that he began writing verses about it on an unfinished letter he'd had in his pocket.

He was released by the British the next day. He returned to Baltimore and wrote more verses, or stanzas, to be sung to the tune of an old English song, "To Anacreon in Heaven."

"The Star-Spangled Banner" was approved by Congress as the national anthem in March of 1931—more than one hundred years later.

SALUTE THE FLAG

People in uniform salute the flag by raising their right hands to their caps. Men and boys without uniforms take off their hats when the flag passes and when they say the pledge to the flag or sing the "Star-Spangled Banner." All people not in uniform put their right hands over their hearts, especially when they say the Pledge.

The Pledge of Allegiance was written by Reverend Francis Bellamy in 1892. The words were changed a bit in 1923 and 1924. It became the official pledge in 1945. Then in 1954, President Dwight D. Eisenhower signed a law that added the words, "under God."

THE PLEDGE OF ALLEGIANCE

(And What it Means)

I pledge allegiance to the flag of the United States of America (I promise to be loyal to my country's flag)

and to the republic for which it stands (and to the government and nation it stands for),

one nation under God (one country that allows each person to hold the belief of his or her choice),

indivisible (one country that cannot be split into parts),

with liberty and justice for all (where everyone is free and has the right to be treated fairly and equally).

FLAG WORDS

banner   flag

bunting   cloth used to decorate, usually red and white stripes and blue with white stars

canton   rectangle in upper corner of a flag near the staff or pole

color guard   people who present the flag in a program or parade

field   background color of the flag—also called the *ground*

flag day   June 14 is flag day because it was on that date in 1777 when the Stars and Stripes became the official flag of the United States of America.

fly   striped end of the flag; also the lengthwise measurement of a flag—We also say a flag *flies* when it's up, especially if the wind or breeze makes it appear to fly.

fold   A special way to fold the flag is shown on pages 12 and 13.

government flag   flag flown over government buildings—In some countries, there is a flag for government and a different one for the people. They are one and the same in the U.S.

half-mast, half-staff	halfway up the flagpole or staff
halyard	rope to which a flag is attached
hoist	to raise; also the measurement of the width of a flag or its canton
honor guard	see *color guard*
national flag	flag displayed by people (private citizens)— See *government flag*.
official code	flag code or rules adopted by Congress in 1942— Before that a flag code was worked out by patriotic groups. Soldiers, sailors, and marines followed a military code. Present code adopted 1976.
peak	ball at top of pole or staff
royal standard	flag that goes everywhere a king goes
salute	respect shown to flag by a hand movement
staff	rod to which a flag is attached and carried or placed in a holder to stand
standard	ball, eagle, or something at the tip of a flagstaff or pole
truck	block at the top of a flagpole, just under the peak—It has holes or a pulley for the halyards.
union	in the U.S. flag, the blue canton—See *canton*.

AN AMENDMENT TO
PROTECT THE FLAG

There have been times in the country's history when people who disagreed with the government have protested by burning or defacing the flag. But some people have tried to protect the flag by making such things against the law.

In 1995 both houses of Congress passed resolutions in favor of an amendment that read:

"The Congress and the States shall have the power to prohibit the physical desecration of the flag of the United States."

On December 12, 1995, the Senate failed to pass this amendment by the necessary two-thirds vote. But a Harvard law professor has offered a second possible wording that is a little clearer. This may some day be offered as an amendment to the U.S. Constitution.

"The Congress and the States shall have the power to prohibit the act of knowingly defacing or burning the flag of the United States."

INDEX

Ruth Shaw Radlauer cannot forget her Girl Scout days when she learned how to *Honor the Flag*. Once in 1989, that Girl Scout inside of her became angry with the way people left flags up in the dark and out in the rain and snow. She decided to write a book about taking care of the U.S. flag.

For many summers, Ruth raised the flag at Girl Scout Camp Sacagawea in the Casper Mountains of Wyoming, but today she lives in California with another author, Ed Radlauer. They have three grown children, David, Robin, and Daniel, a granddaughter named Tracy, and two grandsons, Scott, and Ruben.